THE WE ____
JOINER
DESIGN & BUILD YOUR IDEAL JOINERY BUSINESS

Bruce Poling

Published by

Business Growth Advisors

SYDNEY, AUSTRALIA

To have freedom means you can be present for your family both physically and mentally.

— BRUCE POLING

MDA Publishing
Higginbotham Rd
Gladesville, NSW, 2111
Australia

Book Layout © 2020

The Wealthy Joiner -- 1st ed.
ISBN: 978-0-6487202-9-4

Introduction

The simple pleasure of choosing to have coffee with his wife DURING work hours is one that Bruce Poling decided he couldn't live without. Being present at his children's school events, was also non-negotiable.

For most factory owners, especially joinery business owners, this was not a possibility. And this was certainly true for Bruce. Until something momentous happened. It was the tragic events of 9/11 that stopped his business in its tracks, and all the years of hard work, the weeks and months of long hours became irrelevant.

This led to a new question. What does true wealth actually look like? Saving money, taking risks and all the sleepless nights were now undone by an event totally out of Bruce's control. Now it was time to re-examine what the purpose of the business was for? Could he make changes in the business so that he could have time and money? This book charts the journey Bruce has gone through and the lessons he has learned in his road to true wealth.

This book is a roadmap for every creative, hardworking joinery business owner who wants to have a life, and a business.

Acknowledgements

I would like to thank my beautiful wife Samantha for being the rock in my life that has helped me get to where I am now, my kids Reilly, Stevie and Taryn for keeping things real and all the clients I have worked with over the past 20 years. Working with so many clients who truly want to find better ways to operate a business and find a better life for themselves has inspired me to always want to help people achieve this goal.

I would also like to thank my parents for giving me the moral compass to always know right from wrong and for also giving me the intestinal fortitude to have the courage to always chase my dreams.

About The Author

I am a son, husband, father, brother and uncle. I love finding beautiful campsites by a creek and enjoying the stars at night. I still think I am a great ice-hockey goalie but at 53 it seems my best days are well past me. Still love playing the game as much as I can though.

I am also a bit of a business analysis nut. I can't help myself. Whenever I see a business, be it a cafe or retail store, my brain always starts to work out better ways they can operate. I find that hard to turn off so this is why I coach businesses. I can use my slightly obsessive mindset to help an industry I love.

Having been a cabinetmaker for many years and owning and operating my own business, my natural desire to help others in business is driven from my own experiences both good and bad and a strong desire to help the industry step up into the current methodologies of today.

CONTENTS

Chapter One

THE WEALTHY JOINER

For a lot of people, having a safe, comfortable, secure job is enough, but if you started your own joinery business, that wasn't enough for you. It is likely your dream of having time to pick your kids up from school, have coffee with your wife on Wednesdays and Thursdays, and taking Fridays off to go fishing.

You were a good tradesman and you thought you would be a good businessperson too. You knew a job wasn't going to give you your dream life and you had enough confidence to back yourself and take the leap, the entrepreneurial leap, into a business of your own.

It is high risk to start your own business, to give up job security, superannuation payments, and paid leave, and go out on your own. Many people after five or ten years in business look back and realise they missed out on all of that foundational stuff that secures their future, so it is important to have that as a part of the dream vision.

When we talk about living the dream, it isn't necessarily about sitting on a luxury yacht, sipping piña coladas, but about being able to have the life you want without the pressure of the boss looking over you, or the customers yelling at you. Perhaps you are not doing the things you love as a tradesman either.

I'm Bruce Poling and I run a business that helps joinery business owners just like you to create real wealth. Not just money, but time and freedom too. This book will give you an insight into how you can achieve that in your business. We work with clients all over the globe and they face familiar roadblocks no matter which country they are located in.

It all starts with something very simple, but not always easy to do.

Defining what success looks like for you.

Chapter Two

DEFINE YOUR DREAM

The first step in succeeding in your business is defining what it looks like: defining your dream.

- Why did you take this step in the first place?
- What was the reasoning behind it?

We will then align that with driving you forward in your business.

Was it that you thought you would make more money? Was it more freedom to choose how you spend your time? For a lot of people who start their own businesses, these realities don't eventuate the way they think they will.

For some people it is like Groundhog Day, living the same day over and over. A lot of people I have worked with have been in the business for over 30 years and never made any significant changes in that time to achieve the dream they wanted in the first place. Many of these people didn't add to their skills and knowledge in any significant way once they started their business.

They are likely exceptional tradespeople, but never took an apprenticeship in business. It takes commitment to admit you don't know something and make the effort to gain more knowledge there. The business grinds to a survive pace and they learn how to get by and survive forever. Most of these businesses never fail, they just keep going day after day and find a way to get through without completely shutting down and failing.

For a lot of people, they jump into the business, and in the first two years it is survival of the fittest. They do whatever they can to get new clients, set up shop, build the right team, and it is exhausting and exhilarating. In the first two years business owners are bulletproof and have blind faith their businesses will work. They take more risks in this time, whether it is buying a new machine, or bidding on a risky job, and the failure rate during this time is usually high as well. It is like a bulletproof tank that never stops.

THE GAP

The Gap

If you could carry that same mindset into the third, fourth, fifth, and sixth years, you would be highly successful. But a lot of people get to a point where suddenly they have something to lose, and they start looking at risk as loss, because they look back over the first couple years and think, "Okay, that didn't work out well for us."

WHERE DID THE YEARS GO?

Many people then stop taking risks or taking decisions and get stuck. They get into the third or fourth year and they see risk as something they will potentially lose on rather than seeing the upside of it. This is when the business stops growing and gets stuck in the sand.

Risk Management

Learning how to run a business is a separate skill altogether. It has nothing to do with how to put a cabinet together or how to cut board, it is about managing risk, choosing your niche, and making sure you are profitable. To be profitable you can't be all things to all people.

We have to transition people from the tradesman/technician mindset to the entrepreneurial mindset. What if you were exceptionally good at one thing a large demographic of people wanted? Wouldn't it be better to be exceptional in that one thing? It is difficult for a tradesperson to think about that, as they have been trained in and are good at doing a lot of things.

For tradespeople , when you've built a kitchen, or a piece of furniture, you feel proud of it and want to show other people. One transition businesses owners struggle to make is they don't look at their business as their product. They don't pride themselves on the business they built the same way they take pride in the kitchen or furniture.

When I talk to joinery business owners, I ask them to tell me about their business and what makes them proud about it. They always talk about the stuff they make; the kitchens or other things they built. Very rarely will they talk about the marketing system they built, and how they got four new leads from that system they built for their business. A lot of tradesmen grew up with a father, uncle, or someone else in their family who passed on the desire to work in the field to them, and it is a cultural thing. Once you get off the tools and become a business owner, that is a new thing, and no one is teaching you that new thing.

Your Customer's Experience

While most start their own businesses because they think they will make more money, have more time, and/or be able to make the products they love, unexpectedly, becoming an entrepreneur is a pathway to learning the skill of building a business, which is the secret sauce to help achieve those dreams.

The old saying if you build a better mousetrap, people will beat a path to your door is just not true. There are millions of better mouse traps than the old standard wire one, but no one knows about them. If you build a better mouse trap, people won't beat a path to your door, because if you can't market it, you are the best kept secret in the world and you will go broke. Most tradespeople believe if they just do beautiful work, they will have a successful business, and it can be a big wake-up call when it turns out it is not that easy.

If that were true, there wouldn't be jobs for coaches like me because there would be so many successful businesses we wouldn't be needed. But marketing is important. You need a marketing strategy, a sales strategy, and a website. It is not just about making beautiful stuff.

Running a business is about managing risk, choosing your niche, and making sure you are profitable.

A friend of mine once met James Morrison, probably one of the best trumpet players in the world.
"Why do you think people come to see me play?" James Morrison asked.

"Because you're the best trumpeter in the world," he replied.

"There are only three people in the world who are qualified to know whether I am the best trumpeter, and you're not one of them," he said.

"You're probably right," he conceded.

"You can't tell whether I'm playing the best in the world or am just an average trumpeter," he continued. "The reason you came is because of all of the other stuff that surrounds it. The fun I have on stage, the connection with the audience, the joy that doing my craft gives me."

That stuck with me. Whatever your skill is, whether a musician or a joiner, there are very few people who are able to judge whether you are the best or not. Joiners need to build around their skills and show the whole customer experience, because it's likely your customers can't tell whether what you are making is the very best. But the experience that surrounds your core product they can certainly make a judgement on.

Of course, there is a minimum expectation, like with James Morrison; his music has to sound good at a minimum, but it is how it makes you feel, and only the customer can define that. Too many businesses aren't connected with the customer because they are too busy in their own head about what they are doing and how they are doing it.

In this business many of us say, "I'm going to build our cabinets to the standard I want." But that is over building. That is leaving money on the table. The customer didn't care about that, they cared if you were on time, if you were pleasant on the phone, that you didn't leave a mess in their home, picked up your tools, and were safe.

I didn't pay attention to any of that when I started. I wasn't concerned with the customer's wants and needs, I was engrossed as a technician in what I was doing and what I thought they would want. That was the culture I understood. We were taught to focus on the thing we were doing rather than how it makes someone feel.

Too many
businesses aren't
connected with the
customer because
they are too busy in
their own head

My Story

I remember very clearly when I realised, I didn't want to do it anymore. I didn't know what was next, but I knew this wasn't it.

I started out on a fairly typical path as a tradesman. I worked for someone else, but I don't ever remember a time when I **wasn't** thinking about having my own business. My parents both had steady jobs, my Dad as a metallurgical engineer in a lead zinc smelter, and my Mum in a bank, so I'm not sure where my entrepreneurial spirit came from.

I knew I wanted to own my own business, make my own decisions, and work for who I wanted to work for, doing what I loved doing, but I also knew I didn't know how to run a business. I took a business course through the New Enterprise Incentive Scheme in Adelaide, which I believe still continues today. It was a low-level way of creating a business plan and learning about financials which started my path of business knowledge. I knew I was a good tradesman, so perhaps not every year, but reasonably regularly, I did something to increase my business knowledge.

After several years working in Adelaide in Australia, I eventually ended up with a kitchen manufacturing business, when my wife and I moved to Canada in 1995. We started a new business with my father in a small area with around 25,000 to 30,000 people in it. Within the first couple of years, we captured 50% of the market by setting up our business the right way. We had some very good years, but we had some really tough ones as well.

Although the size and shape of the business changed over the years, we typically had three people in the factory and two installers running around. We manufactured our own cabinets and had a specialised paint booth, so unlike our competitors we did a lot of spraying and polishing in-house. Eventually we also got our team right, which made a huge difference. It was difficult finding people to help me run the business and show up for work, particularly in the small area we lived in.

When the business was going well, I felt myself exhale. I finally felt we could achieve that dream I had in my head all of those years. When I had a lot of work booked, saw the profits coming in every month, and watched our marketing systems being successful, I was filled with pride and a sense of relief that all of the hard work was paying off.

When you have that success, you should sleep better at night and be a better partner, father, and friend, but if that doesn't happen when you achieve business success, you are not achieving true wealth.

The Illusion of Balance

True wealth is different for everyone, but for me it was confidence I was creating a bright future for me and my family. Beyond knowing about that future, I wanted to be living it now. Wealth is not just about money but an internal state of mind. It is about relationships, adventures with your family, and acquiring meaningful things, as well as the results in your business.

Work-life balance is a myth in our industry. The myth is they are two separate things. Most people think that they can leave the stress of work at the door and build a wall between the two. The reality is that if work is stressful or your business isn't doing well, that's going to overflow into your regular life. It's going to effect your leisure time, your partners and your friends and family. The message you get is....don't bring that home. All that does is build up until you eventually explode. If you are a business owner, there is no separation between what you are doing personally and professionally, so we need to find a way to meld the two together. We need to work so our family supports us in our businesses through the good times and the bad, but also to be present for them when they need us.

That is the balance we have to find.

Wealth is not just about money but an internal state of mind

Chapter Three

GAME-CHANGING PROCESS

September 11, 2001 changed everything in our world.

After years of custom designing kitchens and working with people so intimately for such a long time, I burned out. I got overwhelmed and stopped loving it. We also hit the maximum customer base we were likely to get from our small area.

We then decided to change the business model to be solely a manufacture – supply company. We were close to the United States (US) and Canadian border.

Just across the border there were a lot of people designing and installing kitchens, but no one was manufacturing. They were buying from suppliers on the other side of the country. We built relationships with these businesses and started receiving orders. We put everything we had into transitioning into manufacturing and it was paying off.

When September 11, 2001 came along and the planes went into the Twin Towers, everything changed. The US shut down their borders. Prior to this, we could drive 10 minutes to the border and then go down to visit our clients. This turned into a tonne of paperwork and an eight-hour drive to the only commercial border crossing. Our delivery time for products went from one hour to now two days, or not at all if they decided to not let us cross for any random reason, which they did a few times.

This was extremely stressful, and as I was already burned out from the custom kitchen business, I decided I was done with the business. I didn't know what that meant, but I knew I needed to prepare the business for sale, and find something else to do that would make me happy for the rest of my life, or at least for now.

We went back and analysed the business and looked at what happened in the years we did well and also in the years we did not. I realised the common denominator in the periods we did well, was I had a consultant in to help me improve something in the business. When I sat back and thought about it, I had tremendous respect for these people. I realised they were the people doing the things I wanted to do the help the industry.

One such consultant was Norm Starling who was a cabinet maker himself who had a business in the past. We didn't need help with our cabinet making as we were already good at that, we needed help with pricing the work for profitability. Norm taught me a cost-plus pricing system that was one of many game changing processes I still teach others today.

There are lots of businesses where the jobs are profitable, but the business isn't. How did that work? We weren't taking into account all of the overheads. He taught me a system to ensure so your business makes a profit, and I am teaching this system to my clients now.

Transition to Coaching

When I first started coaching other business owners, I knew I wanted to be the best coach in the industry and help as many people as I could. I wanted to pass on the skill and knowledge I knew would really help people in the industry, but I also knew I didn't have enough technical knowledge to be the great consultant or coach I wanted to be.

I went back to school, which in your 30s and 40s can be confronting, and studied with an organisation called APICs. I started with a certificate in production and inventory control management (CPIM). That gave me the technical knowledge I needed to connect the dots of what I already knew and also introduced me to lean manufacturing and all of the wonders that brings to the table. Since then, I haven't stopped learning. I have also gone on to attain professional accreditations in Business Coaching (AIPC) and every year I take on new knowledge which makes me a better coach for my clients.

My coaching business only helps people that run joinery manufacturing businesses, which could be kitchen cabinets, furniture, shop fitting commercial work, benchtops, or even clients who just spray two pack paint and supply to others. Our clients are anything from a small two-man business to those with 50 to 100 employees. Small to medium sized businesses are our sweet spot. We have clients all over the world such as in the United Kingdom (UK), New Zealand, and throughout Australia.

I have a "Dream Team" of coaches who work with me. Hamish, works in the factory improvement fundamentals side of the business and has clients making impressive efficiency improvements in the first couple of months. It is normal to see at the end of 12 months a client he is working with has achieved 40 – 60% gains in efficiencies. Lynda works on leadership, performance, and culture improvement and is getting outstanding results. She has a very special way of helping people remove their personal blocks and create forward momentum they have never had. This outcome results in inspiring others to do the same.

We also offer the services of a a marketing agency because the lifeblood of a strong business in new business. We help them build websites, put marketing strategies together, build social media presence, and so on.

Our team

Hamish Campbell
EXECUTIVE COACH

Hamish has been a valuable part of the TJC team since 2019.

Lynda Tregoweth
EXECUTIVE COACH

We would like to introduce you to our newest team member, Lynda Tregoweth.

Kym Bina
BUSINESS MANAGER

Kym has been holding things together at TJC since early 2019

Freedom

To have freedom means you can be present with your family both physically and mentally. When I ask business owners how many hours each week they work, they typically respond with 50 or 60 hours. Then I ask when they are not working, are they still working? If they respond yes, that means even if they are home with their kids, they are not really there. That is not freedom.

Freedom can mean a lot of things. It might be freedom to take the family on holiday for a couple of months. It might be to get up late because you know your team at work has it sorted. It might mean you have the money to do the things you want. Mostly it means your business is working well enough you can be present and not have to worry about it because you know your team has your back. Freedom is knowing when you are away from your business you have confidence the systems and your team are delivering exactly what you promised so you can be present with your family, or enjoy the moment with your friends, and make the choice about when you wake up in the morning.

You can have a
business you don't
have to carry on
your back all day
long

The Dream Lifestyle

Many people have clear ideas about what they want to achieve whether it is a nice house, car, a jet ski, a fishing boat or whatever the material possessions they might desire. Some people we work with have those toys but they can't really afford them, so they don't necessarily feel good about them. They know eventually it is going to topple over because the payments on them are too high.

Having the lifestyle you want isn't just about the things and objects you want, but being able to afford it comfortably without it affecting anything else in your life. Some people worry having a nice car makes them materialistic which might make them a bad person. It is okay to have nice cars, family holidays or whatever else you desire if you can actually achieve it in a sustainable way. When you know mentally you have earned it and are not just falsely achieving it by way of credit, you will have peace of mind.

We humans are social animals, so our family and other relationships drive almost everything in life. They are an important part of the whole thing too.

Meaningful Work

If someone has wanted to run a business their whole life, they get passionate about being an entrepreneur and their business, whatever they are creating becomes their product. They get passionate about the business and that is how they drive their future going forward. Joiners start out with loving building cabinets, or custom kitchens, or furniture, and this is so ingrained in our DNA it will likely never leave us.

It is difficult to get someone running a joinery business to take time off because they really love what they are doing, and it gives them a sense of achievement and fulfilment. The problem is, if you are in business long enough and it is not successful, you stop loving it, even if you started out doing something you loved. Give it enough time being unsuccessful and it will take away your joy of life itself. It is so important to make sure your business is successful, but equally important to love what you are doing. In this industry the pride in the product needs to be as high as the pride in the business.

When that is all in place, you will have freedom; freedom of time to choose what to do, money freedom to invest in whatever element you want, lifestyle freedom to be present when you are away from work, and the freedom to acquire all the toys and adventures without incurring undue debt. All of this has to be balanced with meaningful work.

Chapter Four

THE COMPONENTS OF A JOINERY BUSINESS

The Right Size Business

When we analyse components of a joinery business, we see elements which repeat across every business. People always talk about growth. "We need to grow our business; we need to grow our business." Many people say they want to achieve this without actually knowing what it means.

We need to define what growth actually means. We tell people not to think about growth all the time but figure out what you want to do with your business and work out how to get it to the right size. We redefine growth as the right size.

Often when I talk about growth, a client will step back and say, "Hang on, I don't want 100 people working for me !" I tell them we are not talking about making the business BIG! We are talking about getting it to the right size so it is sustainable.

How does a business grow? Like a building, you could build the windows, walls and the roof really well, but if the foundation isn't strong, the building will fall over. Your business needs to have a strong foundation before long-term sustainable growth is possible.

For a business to reach the right size, we have to make sure it is stable first. The first key to stability is how you handle your money. It is not about having more, but how you are dealing with your cash. Next is about segregating your time in tasks that are high value. Finally, it is about how you are getting your team to grow your business. Your team is important because you are not going to grow your business, your team will do it for you.

Once the business is stabilized, they we can look at growth or getting it to the right size. Firstly you need a system in your business for organic growth so your business grows each year and keeps up with the trends and competition.

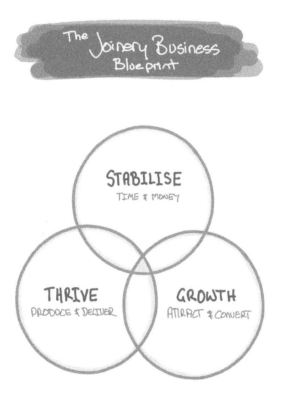

Stabilise Your Business: Time and Money

If you were to take the money you put into this business, say $1 million and put it into a term deposit account with no risk, what would you expect to get back? You would expect around three to four percent or more with ZERO risk! Is the net profit of your business more or less than that? For some of our clients, it is less. We need to get the business giving back far in excess of the risk and effort you are putting into it.

To achieve this, we need to work smart, not just hard. The concept that if you work hard for long enough, everything will come together, is a myth. If it were true, the vast majority of businesses in the world would be wildly successful because every business owner works hard. Businesses have problems because they are not working smart.

"Smart" is something you can learn … just like you did in trade school.

It is not about cashflow, it is about knowing the cash you have and how you are going to manage it. You know the costs of your business; what the costs are for the month. You also know how much you have coming in this month. Where a lot of businesses fail is in how they manage that cash.

The other issue is how you are managing your time.

No one has a time management problem; everyone has a task management problem. You are trying to do too many tasks in too little time you will feel like you don't have any time. You intentionally did too many tasks in the time you had. You can in intentionally change this You have total control over whether you can do more in less time or whether you can manage your tasks better.

The Team Flow

Most joinery business owners grew up in an environment where they were yelled at and taught to "do what you're told." That environment is still strong today. I often ask clients how they feel they about being in service to their team, and that is very confronting for them. Many feel their staff should be in service to them because they are paying THEM!

When you are in "service" to your team, they will get on board to do what you and they want and you will create a close-knit team and great culture that is also in "service' to your customers

Every person that works in your business needs to be really clear about the process you want them to follow. If you create a process and there is a mistake, it is not about them making a mistake, but about the process itself having a flaw somewhere. If you make your business response to mistakes about improving your process, you will improve your people. If you expect them to just know what to do, then you will get all kinds of chaos in your business.

Darren Mckavanagh was a guest on my podcast and discussed his business, The Kitchen Builder. He has achieved the freedom to holiday multiple times a year, going skiing and going on his catamaran boat. He spends very little time in his business but still works ON the business every month. He is able to live that lifestyle while his business supports that. It also supports the people in the business. Darren built a team to support his concept and said it is imperative to meet your teams needs.

If you are in a dark room, you can still get things done. But it's going to be a lot easier with the lights on

Darren focused on his leaders, making sure they were clear in their positions and the "lanes" they needed to stay in. Building internal business systems is also a key to his success.

Darren: Owner of the Kitchen Builder

Core Efficiencies

The team and leaders systematise the flow in the business, creating efficiencies that flow to the core of the business. The business runs very well without him and he is proud of that. He does check in with the business and makes sure everything is ticking over nicely, but he focuses on making sure the business keeps working, not being in the business doing the tasks. His focus is on the people and systems and has created an amazing result.

The turning point for Darren was in the early stages of his career he received a cheque for $20,000. He had no interaction with the client and didn't know anything about the job, he just knew the money came from hissalesperson selling a job. That was his light bulb moment when he realised he could have a business he did not need to carry on his back all day long, he could have a business that was a profitable investment! Once that realisation happened, all Darren then had to do was work out HOW.

He could have a great salesperson getting great results with clients bringing in the money and he didn't need to be a part of it at all. All he had to do was create and grow this thing, which he did, and now he has the business he wants.

Chapter Five

SUPERHERO MONEY MANAGEMENT

We are not born with superhero money management skills, it is something that we can teach you and then you can do it. Managing money is about managing risk, but remember, risk is not always about loss, there is also potential for reward. At the casino, you could lose, but you could also win. We are looking at the win side of things.

Once you get to the stage where you are comfortable with the numbers, let them guide you as they tell you a story. Numbers don't lie. Much like a GPS that navigates your car on the roads to your destination, you tell it where you want to go, (it already knows where you are) and tells you how to get there. Letting your numbers tell you what you need to know to solve your problems is much like using a GPS navigator. Once a month, extract the numbers and look at your profit and loss statement. Don't be afraid of your numbers. Not knowing them is like playing darts blindfolded

About three years ago I had a client whose joinery business wasn't going in the direction he wanted. The pricing wasn't nailed down yet and he was struggling a bit financially.

We helped him with the pricing system to guarantee his business was profitable. We also helped him understand how to analyse the numbers in the business. He then saw the issue stopping his company growing was he didn't have the machinery or automation he needed to be competitive.

MONTHLY
P&L
Analysis

SOMETIMES
P&L
Analysis

NEVER
P&L
Analysis

| THRIVING |
| PROFITABLE |
| GETTING BY |
| BREAK-EVEN |
| BACKWARDS |
| OBLIVIOUS |

Certain
about the
future

Uncertain

Overwhelmed

Once he stabilised the business, he extracted the new numbers i his business was now successfully turning a profit. This gave him the options to buy the new machinery that created the automation and efficiencies at the core of his business.

We have another client who struggled with time management. He always had a huge pile of quotes on his desk he needed to follow up. We helped him prioritise the high value task his day and ask for a decision from this leads during a final quote presentation. This simple change gave him the deal with "objections" right away, close more sales and almost totally eliminate any follow up to do. The result is a massive amount of time back to him each day.

We also looked at the workflow in the factory and created time for some continuous improvements. There is a saying *"it is not about speeding things up but shortening the distances."* If we could shorten the distances between the processes, we could free up time. We created dramatic reduction in lead times in jobs. When you are still producing at the same level, but you have more time, you can devote it to making more improvements in the business.

Grow to The Right Size

The word 'growth' has a negative effect on a lot of people in this industry because they assume it means their business will become too large a business for them to manage. A lot of people in this industry don't want to become a big business. Sometimes you may need a larger premise or to get more employees, but that is not growth, that is getting your business to the right size. This is why I am careful to talk about getting your business to the right size.

Firstly, your business has to grow to where you don't feel the weight of it on your shoulders. When your business is the right size with all the systems working, that weight will come off.

Planned Growth

You may think you have run the last two years at a certain size with a certain number of employees, but it is not getting you where you need to go. You decide to take on bigger jobs, or only take on a certain type of business. We will put a structure in place that will have a beginning and an end planned growth period. It will not continue forever into the future.

Organic Growth

Our organic growth system ensures businesses have the structure and systems to keep up to date with their competition and what is new in the marketplace. If you don't have this in place, in two or three or 10 years, you will wake up and see you don't have the machinery to compete with others in the industry and your business will slip behind.

This is about keeping you competitive and maybe even slightly ahead of the industry, not necessarily growing into something you can't or don't want to manage. Customer demands change constantly and evolve, and unless you're responsive to that, your business will not grow, but decline. If you are staying where you are, everyone else is moving ahead of you and you are actually falling behind and may not be able to catch up. It is extremely overwhelming to find out you are so far behind in business you may not be able to catch up and closing your business might be a reality.

We do need to invest in technology, new machinery, and great talent when it is available. It is important to focus on those areas keeping you competitive. This growth is not about becoming a corporate beast, but about keeping up so you are growing and not going into decline. What size business would help me have a business that takes the load off my shoulders, rather than puts the load on my shoulders?

The fear of growth probably comes from overworked and overstressed business owners who are already working 100 hours a week, not making enough money, and we're telling them they need to grow when they need to do less. What we're saying here is yes, you do need to do less, but you can do that within an organic growth system. And putting these systems in place will take away all that burden.

I recently had a conversation with a client who for months we asked to hire a bookkeeper. He is very reluctant to hand over that task. But we are all very clear he should let go. Bookkeeping is a rudimentary level role in the business, and while important, does not add a lot of value to the business. If we freed up eight hours a week of this business owner's time, would he sell one or two more jobs? That might bring in another $250,000 and have an extremely high impact.

What would he do with that money? He might hire someone to do purchasing or some other things, and then he can see how the business can get to that right size pretty quickly. Once you get to that right size, then it is about whether you want to grow larger and scale what you already have, and do you have the right systems in place, and the right culture to make it happen? Yes, as a business owner you can do all of these things, but there needs to be someone else so you are freed up to do the higher value things for the business.

Trusting the Experts

Making these changes is about trust, and knowing that if you don't change, you will stay stuck. If you make a decision, it might not work out, but then you will try something else that will work. But if you don't start trying things in a different way, you will not get the result you want. If you want to continue working 80 hours a week, which you don't, get your business to the right size, or you will work for 80 hours a week for the rest of your life. That is not sustainable. Eventually you will break, and you might lose everything.

The fear of losing everything is much larger than the fear of trying something new that might not work. For a lot of business owners, delegating key tasks is difficult. They might think they are good at running the pace, purchasing, and entering money into the accounting package, but a good bookkeeper might be way better at this stuff than you. Eventually we have to accept having a business full of individual specialists doing key value tasks in their specific roles will free you up to keep managing the dynamic of keeping all of these functions going.

As the owner you might have a specific role which could be sales or production. Some business owners have a sales team as the owner doesn't like doing sales, so the team does that and the owner focuses on production. It is our particular make up or mindset that fits us into a particular category, but we cannot specialise in all of them. You are either really good at sales because you are comfortable with that because of the type of person you are, or you are more technically-minded and you like to live in the space where you make the stuff after it is sold. If we accept that we are going to live in one of these areas and release the other area to someone who is better than us, the business starts moving forward quickly, and you start getting some of that time, freedom, and wealth you are looking for.

The business needs a leadership team with three people in it; finance, production, and sales and marketing. Each of these roles has different mindsets, but for the business to grow and scale so it is stable and thriving, those three mindsets need to work very well at the same level in the business.

Developing the Right Systems

A system is a series of dependent tasks, or dependent items that are linked together. There needs to be a connection to everything to create a system. If there is a system or communication breakdown, you don't have a system, you have a series of things called silos. Silos don't communicate with each other or are difficult to move from one to the other. When we use the term system, we are saying we want to get all the corners of your business communicating, and all of the data connected so the business is managed in a transparent way.

There is no reason why the data from your sales or production shouldn't be transparent across the entire business. That is not to say the business owner's finances need to be shared, but your system should make information readily available when you need it and where you need it in the system in a way that is easy to use.

The more connected your business can be across the entire chain of departments, the more efficient it will be. For example, if the salesperson has notes they took from a client that they wanted a red benchtop and blue handles, but that lives in their head or on a piece of paper, and production needs that information, that is not a system. If we can connect that system, that data is available to production anytime they need it. Now there is a system of connectivity.

Many business owners we work with work out of an A4 diary where they put in their client notes, quotes and so on. This needs to be put into some sort of electronic system depending on the size and scope of your business. Smaller businesses can cope pretty well with basic Excel spreadsheets; something that puts the data into a place people can access it. For larger businesses, an accounting package like Xero or MYOB that can ideally interact with your other systems is more appropriate. We don't do the double entry ledger system with a piece of paper and calculator anymore.

Our industry needs to realise we are in a modern day. Where we used to take a pencil and write on a piece of paper, now we can take our iPad and write on it which automatically uploads to a folder where someone could actually see the notes. Even if you want to take handwritten notes, there is no reason we can't make that instantly available for someone to access if they want to. It goes to the client folder under initial client notes, uploads as a PDF and away you go. Whether it is writing like this, or uploading spreadsheets, if you are serious about freeing up your time and creating the lifestyle you want, having Fridays off to going skiing with the kids, we have to talk about these things. These are the things that create extra freedom for you on a daily basis.

You can read the note, have someone ask you what you wrote in the note, then have a conversation with them about it, or you can just give it to them. This is time consuming for you and doubles up work.

In my business, we had a lot of handwritten notes. There was a form that needed to be filled out with perhaps 25 entry areas on the sheet. What typically happened was some of the information was collected, but it wasn't always available, or it was on a piece of paper no one could read, or was lost altogether. The job got passed to the next stage before it was ready. In this industry, if we don't get 100% of the information for the detail of the job, it is going to end in tears, full of defects where something is incorrectly installed, and/or is the wrong colour.

We put in a system like in a webpage where you can't hit 'Next' until all of the information is filled out, so the job can't progress without all of the information, and it is collected properly in an accessible database. Recently, a first-year apprentice started a conversation on our Joinery Business Hub Facebook Group where he said he started his first job as a lister. What happens is, the salesperson sells the job, gets all the details, closes the sale, gets the deposit, and signed contracts, then passes it onto a lister. Most businesses don't do it like this anymore, but the lister would check all of the information, then contact the customer if anything wasn't clear or if information was missing.

Now you have two people trying to decipher information rather than one from the source of the information. If the salesperson sold the job and made the customer comfortable and happy they will do the job, the customer leaves happy and trusting the job will be done well. But if suddenly someone else from the company calls and starts asking them questions, they can become concerned.

Have you ever been in hospital getting ready for surgery lying on the gurney sedated and drifting off when the first person comes, looks at your chart and askes if you are allergic to anything? You are thinking, on my wrist it says it right here, and in the chart, you are reading it says I am allergic to penicillin, so why are they asking me this? Then you worry maybe they are going to give you penicillin. You lie there drowsy for another 10 minutes, a different person comes, picks up your chart, asks how you are doing and are you allergic to anything. I have had a few surgeries, and this happened time and time again, and I got more worried how the surgery would go if they didn't know what I was allergic to when it is on my wrist and on my chart.

That worried feeling is exactly what the customer experiences if we don't lock down the details up front, put it into production, and get it right without having to bring them into the conversation again. The lister who started the conversation said the customer got very upset. This is natural because if you are asking questions they already answered, why don't you know? Your system needs to capture the information and pass it thought your system without involving the customer anymore because it creates doubt in your capabilities for that customer. They wonder what the results will be like if we are asking these simple questions, whereas the system should instil trust and confidence.

We work hard to build trust so that our leads are willing to part with their money, and that trust needs to keep going up and up. If your systems are not up to scratch, it will show in different areas and that never ends well. That trust you worked hard to build will erode and getting paid becomes more difficult. You also want referrals from that customer to their friends.

Systems don't need to be complicated. Online cloud access for sharing information in client specific folders is a great place to start.

Next we look at how we crunch the data. When the business gets to a certain size, say over $1 million or more, we start looking at Business Management Systems which encompass everything in one platform. This incorporates your quoting, purchasing, invoicing, inventory, production and so on. In this business, we have already bought automation packages, like for drawing a kitchen in a CAD CAM programming package, we push a button and the machine cuts the parts. We don't have to program it anymore because it is automatically programmed by the software system.

We have already bought into automation at this level, now we need to accept automation at the business level, which is what we do with Business Management Systems. If you don't do it, the burden of labour of people doing tasks, and the mistakes that go along with human errors will make the business implode into itself. You won't reach your goals simply because you haven't automated your business.

About a year before we started working with another client, they bought a Business Management System, but never trained or installed it properly. This was a system we used with our clients as well, but the software alone isn't enough to make systems work. We took our coaching thinking and methodologies, then used the software as a tool to implement them. Once they had better knowledge and understanding of how to use it, their time to quote a job went from two to three days down to 6 hours later. They have since improved on that again.

Once they saw if the job was drawn in the CAD CAM program, it could be extracted into the Business Management System, and the quote done automatically, they cut out almost all of the manual thinking they did before. They also instilled profitability into the business because the system was drawing on their actual cost to buy the product, the actual labour times, and putting it into the price as well. If quoting is the business owner's task, that is a huge time saving. If it is the team, you are making them much more productive to do the high value stuff like talking to clients in the first place.

Pricing

Some Joinery businesses use a linear metre pricing system which is quick and easy, but not really linked to your business costs. Eventually they start losing money due to cost slippage. Other people I work with have a system of spreadsheets they inherited from the original owner that has weird and wonderful ways of crunching numbers they really don't understand because they didn't create the system. When we ask how they would teach their way of pricing to someone else they draw a blank as they don't understand it themselves.

The best was to guarantee profitability is to use a cost-plus system for pricing:

> *[{Material costs + Overhead Markup}*
> *+Labour Costs] + Proofit Markup =*
> *Quote*

Having a system you can teach others easily means the business owner doesn't have to do the quotes all the time, and can go and liaise with clients confident the person doing the quotes will do it well and they will make a profit. Time is finite, so if you are spending two days quoting, you limit the number of jobs you can actually sell. If you can cut that in half, you will have more time to sell more work.

From working with thousands of people in the joinery industry, the general consensus is pricing is a complex, mystical, magical beast, therefore the formula for pricing must be complex, mystical and magical. But when they use these weird and wonderful systems and we look at their monthly profit and loss, often they're still losing money or will be in the coming years

I had difficulty with this back in 1997 when the system I was using wasn't bringing in enough money. I hired a consultant who taught me the proper way to price with a simple cost-plus method and I was blown away at how simple it was. It was the brightest lightbulb moment I ever had and our profits improved because of it

Once I accepted this simple model, within six months our Net Profit turned around by 10%. What do you need to know when pricing a job?

1. *Materials costs are covered – include subcontractors here*
2. *Labour costs are covered – what you pay your employees at an hourly rate plus other employee costs*
3. *Overheads are considered in the overall price – fixed costs like power, heat, marketing etc...*

These are the three areas you spend money on in your business. There are no other areas.

The top things that stop businesses being profitable are:

1. Leaving out overheads in pricing – most business owners are surprised when they see how much their overheads are on a monthly basis.

2. Labour times blow out - not controlling or correctly estimating how much labour the job takes

3. Collecting what is owed to you soon enough

If you have 20% going towards labour, 40% for materials and 30 – 40% of revenue going towards overheads and are making a loss, your numbers are not adding up, and they don't lie.

If you don't set a target for at least 10% net profit, you are losing money on your business investment. Because of your risk, 10% is break even and your target should be 20-25% net profit. This takes a lot of work on your people and systems.

The only three things you should be spending money on in your business are materials, labour, and overhead costs

A lot of people we start working with see their net profit at around three or five or seven percent, and they don't believe they will get above 10% or 15% or 20% because they have never been there.

Marketing and Sales

Not everyone is wired for marketing in this industry. Most of us are wired to be tradespeople and are comfortable in a factory. Some of us are wired for sales, which means we are comfortable talking to people once they are in front of us, but we don't know how to attract them to us. That is just what we know. We don't know about the careful little steps that make us more attractive to customers.

In reality, if you become attractive enough, people will buy from you because they trust you, but if you don't go through that process, selling will always be difficult and awkward.

The typical cycle is someone calls and says they are doing a kitchen, and could we go and measure up? We run around all day measuring kitchens, spending time in someone's home, trying to make us more attractive, go back to our office, then spend days coming up with a quote which we email to them and then pray they go ahead with the job. That is the email and pray method. We are in our comfort zone here, but out of the customer's decision-making process.

If you spend time on your marketing system, before they even make contact, they are already warm and want to buy from you. The difference between someone calling you wanting to work with you, and you hunting down potential customers (you calling them) is night and day.

That is why we create an attraction-based marketing system, so when a customer contacts us, they are actually in the market for what we are selling and want YOU. When your system works, this will happen. When it doesn't they will expect you to sell it to them. Then it is about money and price because you haven't brought any value to the conversation. They will get four other guys to quote then pick the lowest because they don't want you, they just want the lowest price.

There is a big different between them wanting you or wanting your price. The investment in marketing is investing in attracting the right kind of clients for you. You change the paradigm from making a choice based on price to making a choice based on quality and what you, as a business, do best.

A lot of people in our industry have had experiences with poor marketing. They may have tried to boost a post on Facebook or paid a little for online advertising to test the waters, but not had the results. They may have had someone tell them they would get all these wonderful things happening for them, but it doesn't work out. Once they have these bad experiences, they often completely reject any form of marketing, thinking it doesn't work and go back to old school cold calling and word of mouth.

There actually is a great system here which will get results and should go on your profit and loss statement as a percentage of your overheads like heat, light, and power. Your close and conversion rates will go up, dealing with leads is less stressful as they are already coming to you warm or hot wanting what you have to offer.

Marketing may be the most difficult topic I have found over the years to teach to the joinery industry. I think this may be the case for two reasons. 1- Most joinery business owners have no training, education or skills in how to properly market (advertise) what they do and most truly believe that all they need to do is put do good work and the work will just come flooding in. 2- We seem to have a natural objection to anyone selling anything to us. I call it the "hair-trigger BS meter". It seems we have all been sold some system or program that will magically transform our business, which of course never happens, so everyone that comes after gets the "you must be a shyster" treatment.

Even though I have literally 100s of business owners I have helped and I have a genuine place and history in this industry, I still receive this attitude from many people that know nothing about us or what we do. It is one of the characteristics of our industry I love and hate. I love this because you really need to be of high value and be able to prove you are legitimate be of interest, but I hate this attitude because many in the industry dig in too deep and miss out on some amazing things that can truly help them.

Chapter Six

Niche Down Profit Up

Define Your Niche

If you think you are all things to all people, you are nothing to everyone because you are not particularly good at anything, right? If you are not a specialist as a tradesperson, you are not valued highly. It takes courage to narrow down what you actually do. You might not work with builders, you might do renovation work. Or you might do renovation work for Hamptons style homes only. Once you learn the "language" your ideal client speaks, you can target a very specific person and learn how to attract that person. Your niche could be a specific type of person (ie – older people with disposable income) or a product you are well known to make (ie – Shaker or Hamptons style kitchens)

As a business owner, you're not a tradesman anymore. If your focus is on being a tradesman and building all this weird and wonderful stuff, go and get a job and do that. If you want to make this business successful, your business is now your product. Doing weird and wonderful things all the time will not make your business successful. You need to have at least one niche you are known for. You can do other things as well, but you first need to start with one thing you are really good at and become known for, then you can start doing the same thing in another niche, and then another niche. What you will find when you have massive success with one, you are less likely to feel the need to spread into multiple niches. In fact, when you have massive success in one, you will have no time to chase others, and this will be a very good thing for you and your business. While as a tradesperson you might like to make a kitchen today, a free-standing piece of furniture tomorrow, then go frame up a wall the next day, it doesn't make good business sense.

Learn how to attract your niche customer

You can't speak European, but if you want to attract people from East Germany for example, you need to speak the East German dialect. Once you can speak their language, they recognise you as part of their tribe and someone they accept.

Converting Your Customer – The Sales Process

To convert the majority of your leads into paying customers requires a sales process. A missing foundation, or system, I find from most joinery business is a well-documented sales process. Just as we need to assemble a cabinet the same way ever time to both gain efficiencies and achieve a known outcome, the same is true for your sales process. Most business owners have never had any formal sales training so they approach every lead differently every time. It is true every lead is a different person, but if they are an "A" grade lead, we want the same outcome for each of them.   This is for them to convert into a paying customer.

The lack of a sales process most often results in the potential lead creating their own process and taking over the process for you. You will hear it when this happens because they will say things like "thanks .. I will get back to you, or "I will talk to my wife about this" , or " I can give you 50% when you have built the kitchen and the rest when we are happy". These statements are all red-flags to tell you that you are letting the tail wag the dog and you are in for a bad experience. This is all easy to solve when you define the steps in your sales process and simply invite your lead to the "next step" in the process. This also means you are never selling your stuff … what you are selling, if anything, is the next step in the process.

Delivering an Impeccable Product

Delivery on the work we do is not as big a problem as we think it is. Most joinery business owners are great tradespeople, so they already know the "how" to do this. It is the things stopping them from creating great process that is the actual problem. The word "process" is the big one here one. Most often we believe that if we hire "good people" we can just leave it up to them to do the work and when things go wrong in any way we blame them. This is the problem rather than a solution. The solution is to create a great process first that your people will be required to follow. When things go wrong we simple look at the process they we following and make improvements there.

When you improve your process, you will improve your people.

The production of joinery itself will be covered in much more detail in my next book, however I will outline some of the common areas to look at if you want to improve your joinery manufacturing processes.

1. Create a written process for everything you do in your business. From receiving goods to operating the cnc to loading the truck. Ask the people doing these task to

document the processes as, after all, they are the experts in those tasks. If you have not already done this, you will find some amazing results in this simple task alone. It will take some time to do. Could be many months or even a few years but once you have your processes documented you can then look at improving them

2. Make sure you have the right skills (people) doing the right tasks. All too often I find a team of highly skilled tradespeople in a factory doing basic rudimentary tasks ie – running a cnc, or edgebander or even screwing square boxes together all day long) and what happens most often is they either get bored and leave or they create friction with each other because they all believe their way is the best way of doing things. Can you image 5 Gordon Ramsays running a kitchen? The best teams I see in joinery production are the ones with the right people doing the right tasks. You may need one or more high skilled tradespeople, but it unlikely you will need everyone to be

at that level. In fact, the more you can simplify your processes, the more scalable and friction free your business will be.

3. Always look at continuous improvements. We all know the Kodak story where they got stuck when they refused to change and adapt to the digital innovation and the result is a total collapse of a massive business. Our industry has seen some massive innovations in the past 10-20 years with flat-bed CNC machines taking over for panel saw/beam saw to point -to -point CNC machines and this has created some massive efficiency gains and cost reductions. It has also meant we do not need to pay fully qualified tradespeople to run the entire factory. There are literally 100s and 100s of good people available all around you that are perfectly capable of following the proceses you create for them to operate a CNC or feed parts into an edgebanded all day long and all they want in return is a good job. They are not looking to use the skills they have spent 4

years learning in an apprenticeship since they did not do that. They only want a good job in a good place with fair expectations.

4. Shigeo Shingo was a leader at Toyota and is identified as one of the founders of what we know today as "Lean Manufacturing". One of his great words of wisdom is to approach your work this way and in this order:

    1. Look to make a task **EASY** first

    2. Then look to make the task **BETTER**

    3. **FASTER** - Improving the process, or finding ways to have your parts processed faster (creating better flow) without needing your people to speed up

    4. **CHEAPER** – By reducing operating costs we will increase profits. This will lead to a stronger business. By starting with "Easy" then on to "Better" then "Faster" you will find cost

will go down, quality and productivity will go up.

The specific sequence above flies in the face of how most business owners approach things. The will more often go – 1- Cheaper, 2- Faster, 3- Better then 4- Easier .. resulting in no profit to begin with, and production being forced to do things too fast. Creating too many mistakes and errors with no time to improve anything because all the time is spent either making stuff or remaking stuff to correct mistakes … and this is definitely not "Easy"!

5. Be willing to collect the details of the mistakes and errors being made and make time to find the "root cause" of the problems. Most problems were not created where they are found and you will never be able to solve the problem at the same level it was created at. What this means is, if you do not obtain a higher level of knowledge on "how" to solve the problems they will keep reoccurring.

Recruitment

Being able to recruit great people is much like your marketing strategy. A lot of people complain they can't find good people. When I hear that, I ask them to physically look at what their business looks like, and does that impact whether a "good person" wants to work there. When you work in your business all day long, you probably think it is great, and it probably is for you. You have these great people who know internally what is going on, but externally if someone comes in, they look at things from a different perspective. Too often I am talking with a business owner in their factory that is full of scraps and off-cuts, stuff piled everywhere and no order to it, and they are telling me they just can't find "good people". When I ask them if they walked in here for the first time would they want to work here. This is often taken as a personal attack when it is really just some good, eye opening advice and an opportunity to see the real problem.

Often, we complain we can't attract the right people, when in actual fact, we are not accepting we are not attractive to the right people. That's why we can't find them. If we want to hire great talent, we have to be attractive to that great talent. We have to be at that level otherwise we only attract the people at the level we're at all the time.

Chapter Seven

From Survive to Thrive

.

The Nine Foundational Elements

Imagine you have nine foundational elements of your business and they are spinning plates that all have to keep spinning or they will all fall over. Kodak let one of those plates fall over: innovation. They thought digital photography was a fad that would pass. They completely dropped the ball on innovation while all the other plates spun perfectly. But each of those foundations can take the whole business down if one of them falls. When you are thriving, you have all nine foundations of your business like spinning plates, and your job is to run between them and constantly keep them spinning.

The Joinery Business Audit

To get to that point you have to work hard to get those foundation points working. In a thriving business we are constantly focusing on those and adjusting, changing, and improving upon those areas.

There are two critical things that all businesses need to be successful.

1. The ability to leverage other people's time and money

You have probably learned how to leverage other people's time and money with hiring employees, running accounts, borrowing money from time to time, and so on.

YOUR Joinery Business Audit

	focus A	focus B	focus C
MONEY FLOW	Hidden Cash	Cash management	Costs
TIME FLOW	Roles	Delegation	Ideal Week
TEAM FLOW	Team Knowledge	Nurture Creativity	Innovation
MARKETING SYSTEM	Attract	Niche	Brand
PRICING SYSTEM	Cost Plus	Estimate vs Quote	Production info
BUSINESS SYSTEM	Communication	Connectivity	Simplicity
FACTORY FLOW	Create flow	ERRORS	Standardize
PRODUCT MIX	Wants vs Needs	Can-Do Now	future focus
CUSTOMER EXPERIENCE	Expectations	Map Joinery	Feedback system

2. The ability to SCALE

If your business doesn't have the ability to scale, you're in trouble. For example, built-in joinery has an inherent inability to scale. You don't have control over your start date; you have 50 subcontractors there before you who will blow out your dates. Your production is always crippled by that. If you do renovation work, it is somewhat better, but you have invested in this massive manufacturing facility that could do other things. It could produce dog beds, office furniture, Alfresco kitchens for people's decks, and so on, that don't have the same ties to built-in joinery and an installation date.

The Product Mix

We need to have a close look at a business' product mix in its manufacturing facility. Most people think they are a tradie when they run a cabinet-making business. They're not a tradie, they're a manufacturing business. The tradie part is perhaps someone on the bench, but mostly people doing the installation work. Ninety percent of the business is manufacturing

Do not necessarily do what you love all the time, because what you actually want is a thriving business. Sometimes that means we need to add some products to your mix to fill the holes.

Now more than ever in history we are spending more time in our houses. There is a wonderful opportunity to start making things that don't rely on installation dates and things like that. There is an opportunity to start building some really cool stuff in a new way.

I had a customer a few years ago that ran a shop fitting business for commercial shop fittings. It was a fun business, but inherently difficult as start dates were always being chopped and changed. One day he got a contract from a company in Perth to build climbing walls for children's play areas. The contractor would send them a job file with a jigsaw of puzzle parts he would put on a CNC and start cutting, then put it on a pallet and ship it away.

The global pandemic presents unparalleled opportunities for our industry. People are spending more times in their homes than ever before.

This opened a whole new door as this was a wonderful product with no issues of start dates, and he became a specialist for these kids climbing centres this guy would put together on his own. This meant with his shop fitting work, he could start saying no to jobs he didn't really want because he had this other revenue source. Then I asked him what he really would love to be doing, what his genius zone was.

He was in a rock band and knew a lot of other bands who often said it would be great if people could make custom sets for them. They like their microphones a certain height, their speakers at a certain level, their drum kits at certain heights for certain things, and so on. He had thought about it for years, but now with the income streams stabilized in the other two areas, he was free to pursue this and created a whole new business just from his friends with bands.

Finding a Flow in Your Factory

Picture the flow of your factory like a garden hose with a series of valves that live at different stages. Sometimes there are kinks in the hose which need to be smoothed out. Sometimes the valves are closed and sometimes they are open. Your job is to create flow consistently between those valves, opening and closing them, because sometimes they are wide open, but there's nothing going to them, so you want to restrict that.

Our industry is dominated by a tradesmen mindset where projects go through step one, step two, step three, step four, and so on. In other parts of the world, we have already transitioned into a manufacturing mindset. Manufacturing a kitchen cabinet or joinery doesn't need tradespeople for the most part.

Flow means that some things should never stop moving. If you are making parts really quickly, only to pile them up on a pallet and have them sit for two or three days, you are not creating flow. Flow means we start from an end date and work backwards. Often people start too soon or too late, neither of which creates flow. The book called *The Goal* by Eli Goldrat introduces the *Theory of Constraints*. It goes into great detail on knowing your constraints and how to relieve them to create flow.

Flow means that things should never stop moving in your factory

In our industry we are not focused on stopping defects occurring, but finding defects and fixing them. That means we are paying someone to make mistakes, then paying someone to find them all day, and doing nothing to prevent them from happening in the first place. We didn't have flow because we didn't trust the drawing and didn't trust what we assembled, so we had to set it up and redo it again. This non-value-added work goes through the roof.

Value is anything the customer will pay money for. If you say to the customer part of their price is to cut board, they will agree with that. If you tell them part of your price is for me to walk back and forth through the the factory all day long, they will say no, that's your overhead. When you have a process with too many non-value-added steps in it, you will never make profit and it will never flow.

We map out all of the hundreds of actual tasks in a business and break them down into value-added tasks and non-value-added tasks. We do this in manufacturing as well as in the business. We ask the business owner what percentage of time their business spends on non-value-added tasks. They typically put it at around 80% value added. The reality is, most have around 10-20% value-added and 80-90% non-value-added.

When we focus on reducing or eliminating the 90% of non-value-added tasks, that directly impacts profit. Anything that comes out of costs goes directly into your profit. A $1 reduction of costs is $1 into your profit. In Australia many statistics indicate the average manufacturing worker spends up to a total of six weeks per year doing nothing other than walking around looking for work instructions, or their tools or materials.. This is something you can easily improve by implementing many of the things I have outlined in this book.

When you learn more about creating "Flow" in your factory and reducing the waste in your process you will go back to your factories and look at them with fresh eyes. Your staff will look at the bench they worked at for years that was 10 metres away from the next bench, and move them closer together rather than walking back and forth all day long. All of a sudden it is about shortening distances, not speeding things up. If we think we will walk faster between the benches, that won't get you where you need to go.

The Factory Flow Matrix

We are never going to create flow in a factory when day by day and week by week we are putting something new or different into the factory we have never done before or haven't done for a long time. If there is a massive amount of variation in the work going through the factory, or the work is not detailed or well known, there will be problems. On one extreme, you can be a generalist, doing a lot of weird and wonderful stuff that is different every single time, and on the other, you are niched with a select product range you know exceptionally well that flows through your factory without any problems.

We know that customers will be happy with us if we deliver what they expected from us to the standard they were looking for. We do that by being able to repeat the same thing over and over without exception. Meeting customer standards is one of the challenges.

You can be a generalist and still supply a good product and have happy customers, but you won't get the price you want. Most people in the industry can do kitchens of any size and any style, whatever you want, because they are a generalist. People in the industry get upset saying everyone buys on price. The reason they buy on price is the value you offer them is not high enough for them to pay more in the first place because you are a generalist. You can be in this space, but I suspect most people wouldn't want to be.

We see more unhappy customers with generalists because they are doing something new and different every time, so there will be defects, which if they are bad enough, will lead to unhappy customers and low cash. It leads to either low cash, or too many defects.

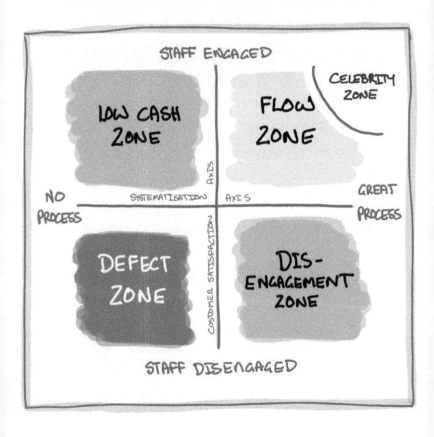

Customers can still be unhappy whether you are specialist or niche, which comes back to why they buy from you in the first place. Are they connected with your business? You could build the most beautiful product in the world, but if you don't build a relationship with the customer, there's no connection. It might start with a small thing like you showed up 10 minutes late for work, or you didn't clean up after yourself properly at the end of the day. Being disconnected can come from not listening to their needs and wants or possibly even working for the wrong customers.

What you want to say is, we've got happy customers, we're a specialist, we've done a great job with our marketing, our message is congruent with what happened, when they met with the salespeople the messages were the same, and we connected. We make a beautiful product, we've got great systems, and even if something goes wrong, we are on top of it. We are transparent about it, the customer knows 100% doesn't exist, but if something goes wrong we will deal with it and not blame them for it.

When you become a specialist, you can move into the "celebrity" zone for that product. Not necessarily being on television but being top of mind or the go-to person for that thing they want. If you are the celebrity in this area, people will come to you for it, or they will ask their friends who will send them to you because you are the best people for shaker style kitchens in that area. Once you are in the celebrity zone, you have choices, can charge a premium for your product, and the customer is happy to pay it.

Where is your business on the matrix? This book and the work we do is all about getting you into the Flow Zone. Once you are there, that is where true wealth comes in; having a profitable business, living the life you want to live, attracting the kind of workers you need, and working with the kinds of clients you want - that gives you back your freedom.

When you become a specialist, you move to celebrity status

The Customer Mix

If your customers are having a bad experience, that can really cripple your business. The customer's experience from start to finish is paramount as they can refer you to people like them. You want to build a relationship with them because "birds of a feather flock together." They will have friends or people they mix with who are like them and you want the opportunity to be introduced to them. You want them to have parties and say, "Look at my beautiful kitchen I got from Bob Jones kitchen maker!" If they are proud of the place they got it from, they will tell others, but if they are not, they will steer them away.

Another problem for some business owners is working with the wrong customers. They cold call and try to sell them then take on work they don't want to do and don't love doing, so it ends badly. Some people get in this cycle and stop enjoying their work.

Working with us

We believe no one really wants to be coached or told what to do. People want solutions to problems and to know they are working with people who can help them solve those problems.

For us to work together you need to know two things:

1. You have a problem that you want to solve with some urgency

2. You know **we** can help you solve the problem you have

Every person we work with needs to know these two things so that when we do begin working together we can do so with no barriers or restrictions and can begin helping you grow and thrive as quickly as possible

You may not feel you have urgent problems right now or you may feel you can work it out on your own. This is perfectly Ok and many people are able to learn and make improvements on their own. The harsh reality is though, if you do not possess the knowledge you need to get you to the next level, you will need to get that knowledge from somewhere. Much like when you did your 4 year apprenticeship to learn how to become a tradesperson, business knowledge and skills are like any other new thing you can learn.

We have a team of coaches specialising in different areas as no one coach has all of the specialist skills you will need in business. We start by asking what you need help with, how the business works and then put a plan together.

Our job is also to help you stay competitive, thriving, and profitable. We research the trends in the industry so you can stay ahead of the game year on year. Our job is to stay ahead of new and innovative ways to help joinery businesses stay competitive and thriving. For example, many years ago we helped people build massive carts all the parts would go into. Now they're making roller systems to get the parts flowing and not using carts at all, or if we use carts, they are small carts that are always moving. But when carts were introduced, it was a huge revelation. We thought the cart was going to be the best thing in the world and it was at the time. When we switched to the roller system getting the parts flowing and completely ditched the carts, that was a huge revelation as well. We know next year there will be something different, we just don't know what it is yet. Our job is to find that thing and bring it to you.

We have different levels of interaction in our programs, so if you are a smaller business it is different to if you are a larger $10 million business.

When I was in business, the best years for me were when I had outside help of some description whether it was financial or technical.

Most people who run a joinery business did an apprenticeship for four years which is how you became an amazing tradesman, but most people running a joinery business I talk have absolutely no formal education on how to run a business. We help with a kind of apprenticeship program to learn the skills, knowledge, and expertise to run your business. You are looking at a tool bag on how to run a business, and that tool bag is empty.

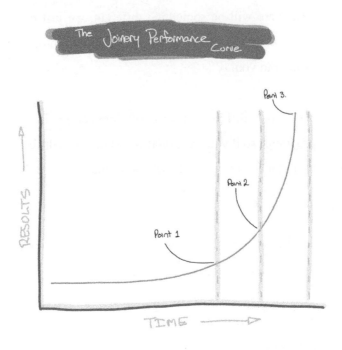

There is no knowledge you have gone out intentionally and brought into your world. We arm you with a new set of skills and tools so you can make good business decisions to grow your business that you know you currently don't have.

We also connect you with a community of non-competitive people going through the same struggles, challenges, and joys. Being in business can be very lonely, so having the support from a community you can lean on is very useful. You don't know what you don't know, but you can't knock on your competitor's door and say, "Hey mate, can you tell me what you're doing?"

In our community you can do that. We can connect you with people from all over the world. These people can willingly openly share their experience with you. Not necessarily the private stuff, but we're talking about an industry we love and want to grow. Our community is a group of people on the same journey with the same ups and downs sharing experiences and helping each other work through them.